Sharing Through Primary Songs

I Am a Child of God

Volume Four

by
Alison Palmer

HORIZON PUBLISHERS
Springville, Utah

ISBN: 978-0-88290-831-1

Published by Horizon Publishers, an imprint of Cedar Fort, Inc., 2373 W. 700 S., Springville, UT, 84663
Distributed by Cedar Fort, Inc., www.cedarfort.com

Cover design by Nicole Williams
Cover design © 2007 by Lyle Mortimer
Edited and typeset by Erin L. Seaward

Printed in the United States of America

10   9   8   7   6   5   4   3   2   1

Printed on acid-free paper

sharing through primary songs

I am a child of god

volume four

contents

Acknowledgments

Many thanks to Duane and Jean Crowther of Horizon Publishers, for continuing to have faith in my work. Great appreciation is extended also to my Cedar Fort family for allowing me to share my enthusiasm for this project with them.

I would like to thank Debra Stinson as well for her dedication and hard work creating the beautiful illustrations that add so much to my words.

I express thankfulness and love to my husband and children for loving me despite it all and for picking up all the pieces of life that I let slide while I'm engrossed in a manuscript.

Most of all, I must express my love and gratitude to my Heavenly Father. He continues to bless me. He filled my soul with the thoughts and ideas that became this book. Through His inspiration, may the lives of many children be blessed.

how to use this Book

Most of us have traditionally separated sharing time into a short lesson and a music time. We have been asked by the General Primary Board to use the full thirty to forty minutes for sharing time; music is integrated throughout. (See "Instructions for Sharing Time," *2008 Outline for Sharing Time and the Children's Sacrament Meeting Presentation,* 1.) This is not always easy. Compliance requires early preparation and more communication and cooperation between presidencies and choristers, but it works!

Music teaches where words fail, and if we do not merge the two, we are missing beautiful opportunities to teach our children things they will always remember. The overall goal of sharing time should be to teach the gospel and build testimonies. *Sharing Through Primary Songs Volume Four* works on this philosophy. Children must first hear the gospel and then sing the gospel. When these two work together, our children will feel the Spirit and know the gospel is true.

This manual is designed to help those who desire to follow the guidance of our leaders to the best of their ability. However, it has limitless potential. The lessons are built around inviting the Spirit through the use of scriptures and song. Please feel free to mold these lessons to fit your needs as a leader, teacher, or parent.

The lessons in this volume are intended to supplement special occasions that need to be addressed in your Primary. There are two lessons for each topic. One lesson teaches the message of one specific song. The second lesson reinforces the topic through multiple songs. Complete instructions, lists of materials, and illustrations are included with each lesson for your convenience.

Please also keep in mind that this is copyrighted material intended for use within the purchaser's home or Primary only. If you enjoy using it, share the information with your friends, but allow them to show honesty by purchasing their own copy of this manual.

May the Lord bless you in your endeavors to serve His children.

1. I Am a Child of God

Children's Songbook, 2–3

Opening Song: "Teach Me to Walk in the Light," *Children's Songbook,* 177
Closing Song: "I Am a Child of God," *Children's Songbook,* 2–3

Lesson Purpose

"I learned of and accepted Heavenly Father's plan. I have a divine destiny" (*2008 Outline for Sharing Time and the Children's Sacrament Meeting Presentation, 3*).

Materials Needed

- Copy, on cardstock, of the sign language illustrations from this lesson

Preparation

- Laminate all illustrations for durability.
- Become familiar with the included sign language gestures for this song. Note that all the words are not included and should not be signed. Those who communicate through sign language are not necessarily concerned with using correct grammar. Sign language is a beautiful expression of thoughts and ideas. This is meant only to be a child's first introduction to that world of beauty.

Teaching Suggestions

This is a much-loved Primary song that will most likely be familiar to most of the children. You might want to have them sing it one time through to engage them in the message of this special song before teaching the concepts and signs that they will learn.

Begin with your own testimony of the special message you will be reviewing with the children. Help them understand how much the Savior and Heavenly Father love them and want the best for them. Remind them that each of us lived with Heavenly Father before we came to this earth. Invite the children to share what they know about the plan of salvation. Emphasize Heavenly Father's desire for each of them to learn and to grow, to become like Him and to return to live with Him again.

We are all Heavenly Father's children, and we all have special gifts and talents that can bring us closer to Him. Ask the children to share some of their own talents and things that make them each unique.

Sometimes the things that make someone special aren't always easy for others to understand. As we learn about ourselves, we can also learn to understand others around us.

Today the children will learn a different way to share the special message of "I Am a Child of God." Those who are unable to hear use sign language to communicate thoughts and feelings to those around them. The children will learn a few of the signs that would be used to "sing" this song with their hands.

Begin teaching the children the chorus. Then move through the verses. Review each phrase with the children, briefly discussing the message of the phrase with the children. Then demonstrate the corresponding signs for that phrase. Let the children copy your movements and repeat the words out loud until the children are comfortable with them.

Invite reverent children to come forward and find the picture representations for the signs they have learned and place them in order on the board. When a word is used more than once in a verse, refer the children back to its original placement.

When an entire verse has been learned, sing and sign it all together. Return the symbols to the bottom of the board, and repeat the process with the other two verses.

After all the verses have been taught in this manner, turn all the sign language symbols over, and mix them up. Invite a reverent child to choose one illustration. The child should demonstrate the chosen sign language gesture for the rest of the Primary children. Invite the Primary to guess what the represented word is. After the word has been identified, take it a step further and have the children identify a phrase from the song that uses the word. Sing and sign the phrase again before choosing a new gesture to identify.

Close by singing the song in its entirety once again, and share your testimony. Be mindful of the Spirit as you sing, and help the children identify its presence, testifying of the truthfulness of the concepts the children have learn about.

I/me/my

child

God/Him/He

sent

here

given

home

parents

kind

dear

lead/guide

walk

help

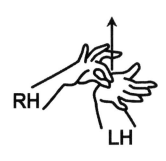

find

way

Teach

must

Do

live

someday/once more

needs

great

understand/learn

words

before

too late

blessings

in store

will

2. Choosing Happiness

Opening Song: "I Need My Heavenly Father," *Children's Songbook,* 18
Closing Song: "Smiles," *Children's Songbook,* 267

Lesson Purpose

"Heavenly Father gave me agency. I chose to follow His plan" (*2008 Outline for Sharing Time and the Children's Sacrament Meeting Presentation,* 2).

Materials Needed

- 2 copies, on cardstock, of each illustration and song title from this lesson
- Chalkboard or other display area
- Tape or other fastener

Preparation

- Color, cut out, and laminate the illustrations and song titles for durability.
- Tape the illustrations and songs face down (in a random order) in a grid on the display area.

Teaching Suggestions

Explain that before we came to this earth we made a choice to follow Heavenly Father's plan. This plan is sometimes called the plan of happiness because Heavenly Father truly wants us each to be happy. Have the children briefly highlight what they remember about Heavenly Father's plan and our part in it.

Heavenly Father gave us the gift of agency on this earth so that we could continue to make choices. He provides us with guidance—like the commandments—to help us make choices that would help bring us great happiness. He also provided a Savior to help us make up for those times when we don't choose wisely. Encourage the children to use their agency to make those choices that will bring them closer to Heavenly Father and give them the greatest happiness in this life.

Invite the children to help you identify some of the things we have been given that will help us be happy and will help us get back to our Heavenly Father. The children will be given opportunities to make choices to see what some of these things are and to sing "happy" songs.

Play a memory game. Pictures match with pictures, and songs with songs. Call one child at a time to choose two cards from the board. When the two chosen cards do not match, turn them face down again. When the two cards match, leave them turned face up for the Primary to see. For the picture matches, discuss how the item pictured brings us happiness and shows that we are following Heavenly Father's plan. For the song matches, sing the songs with the children.

Close with your testimony of the happiness the gospel has brought into your life, and express your gratitude for the gift of agency.

Pictures and Messages

Baby—We came to earth to get a body, to be tested, and to make choices that would help us learn how to be more like our Heavenly Father.

Family—Heavenly Father placed us in families so that we could learn and grow together. This was part of Heavenly Father's plan for us.

Temple—We go to the temple to learn more about Heavenly Father and His plan. At the temple, we make promises to Heavenly Father to do those things that will make us happy and help us return to Him. We can be sealed to our families in the temple so that we can always be together.

Baptism—We can be washed clean of all our sins and promise Heavenly Father that we will try to be like His son, Jesus Christ. When we are baptized, we become members of Heavenly Father's Church and show Him that it is important to us to continue to learn about Him.

Word of Wisdom—When we follow the Word of Wisdom, we keep our bodies healthy and clean. This lets us run and play and feel better everyday. When our bodies are clean inside and out, we are showing Heavenly Father that we respect the gift of our bodies and that we want to take care of them.

Sacrament—Every week when we take the sacrament, we can remember the covenants that we made when we were baptized. We think about Jesus Christ and all that He has done for us so that we could repent and remain spiritually clean. We make promises to try our best every day to choose the right and to fix things that we have done wrong.

Commandments—Heavenly Father teaches us how to live the gospel. He gives us rules, or commandments, that help us stay safe and understand Him better. We learn to be more like Heavenly Father when we keep His commandments.

Jesus Christ—Heavenly Father knew that we would make mistakes sometimes, even when we were trying our best, so He sent Jesus Christ to live on the earth. Jesus shared His example of how to try our best to keep the commandments and to serve Heavenly Father. He also atoned for all of our sins. He paid the price for our mistakes, and He promises to wash them away if we repent. He made it possible for us to return to our Heavenly Father.

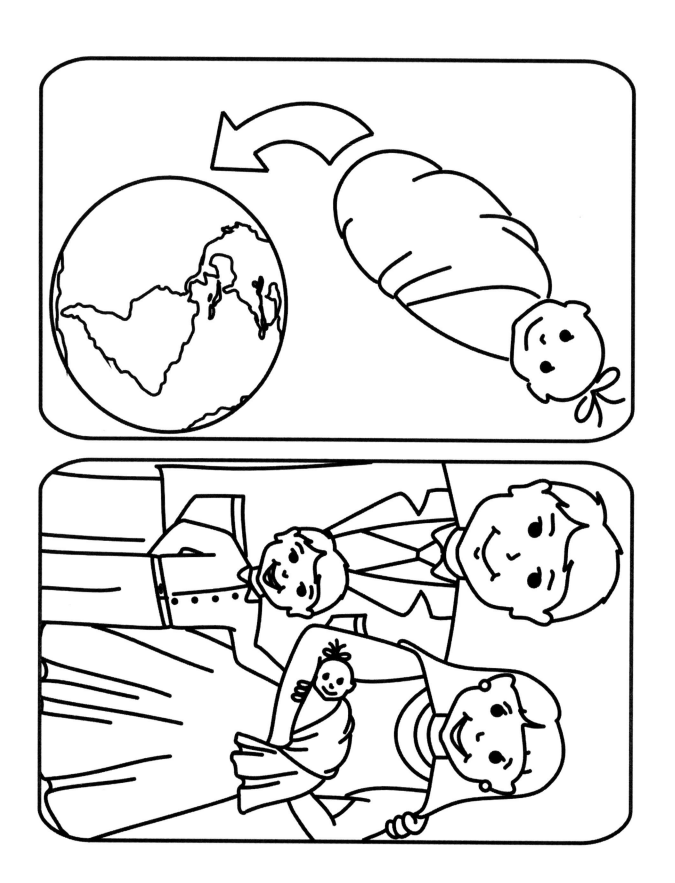

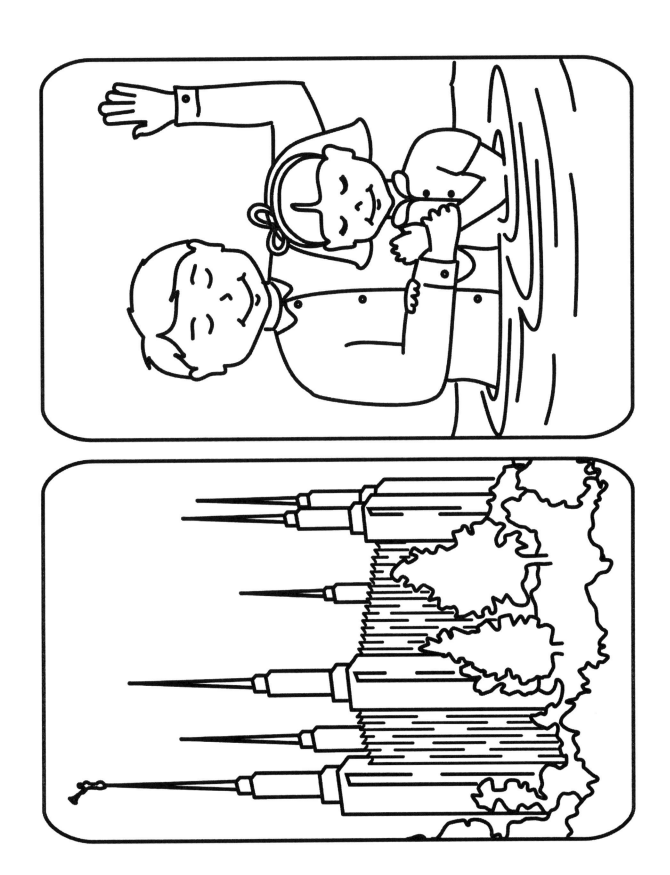

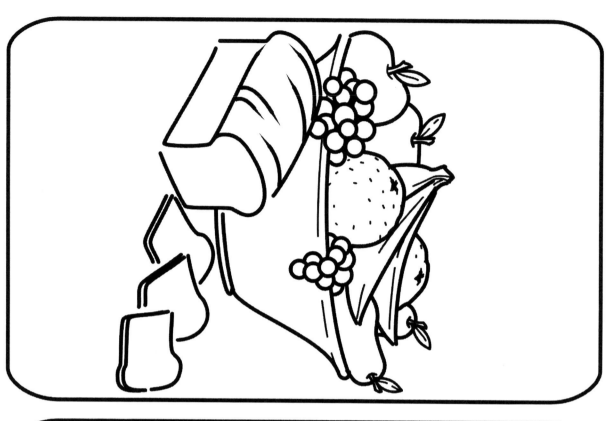

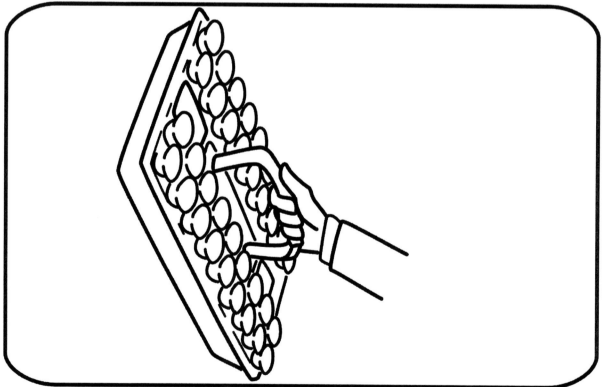

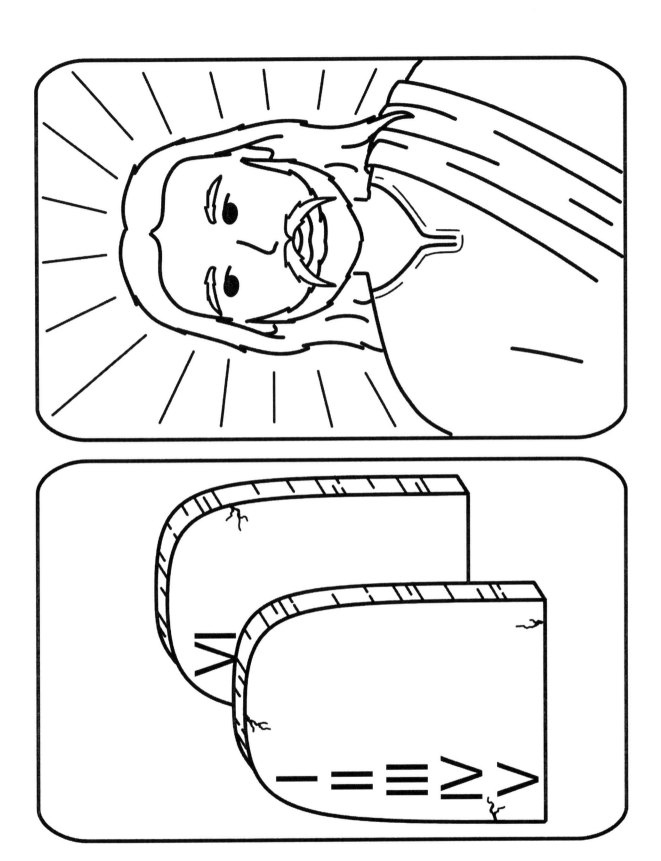

I Lived in
Heaven

CS pg. 4

I Am a Child
of God

CS pg. 2

I Know My
Father Lives
CS pg. 5

I Will Follow
God's Plan
CS pg. 164

Happy Song

CS pg. 264

Jesus Wants Me for a Sunbeam

CS pg. 60

If You're
Happy
CS pg. 266

Choose the
Right Way
CS pg. 160

3. Tell me the stories of Jesus

Children's Songbook, 57

Opening Song: "I Think When I Read That Sweet Story," *Children's Songbook, 56*
Closing Song: "Tell Me the Stories of Jesus," *Children's Songbook, 57*

Lesson Purpose

"The Bible and the Book of Mormon testify of Jesus Christ" (*2008 Outline for Sharing Time and the Children's Sacrament Meeting Presentation, 4*).

Materials Needed

- Copies, one for each child, of the word prompt page from this lesson
- *Gospel Art Kit (GAK)* no. 212, 214, and 322
- Crayons or colored pencils

Preparation

- Cut apart the word prompt page on the lines.
- Staple the pages together in order of the song words.
- Be familiar with the scripture stories associated with the *GAK.*

Teaching Suggestions

Show the children the title page of the Book of Mormon. Help them understand that one of the main purposes of the scriptures is to help us learn about and gain a testimony of Jesus Christ. All the stories that the scriptures tell help us learn more about the Savior and the gospel.

The children will learn a song today that describes stories from the scriptures. Use the *GAK* to share the three scripture stories in the order that they are described in the song. Help the children understand where in the scriptures these stories come from and what they can learn from them.

Introduce the words to each verse after telling the corresponding story. Help the children make the association between the story they just heard and how it is described in the song. Repeat the words to each verse with the children several times, and try singing the verse once before moving on to the next story and verse.

After all three verses have been reviewed in this manner, shuffle the pictures, and have the kids put the stories back in order as they are told in the song verses. Review all the words again, and sing the song in its entirety.

Express to the children that the scriptures are full of stories about Jesus Christ because people and prophets took the time to write down how they felt about Him and what they had learned from His life. Each of us can do the same thing by keeping journals of our own stories and testimonies.

Invite the children to create their own storybook prompts for this song. Hand out the small prompt booklets to the children. Ask the children to draw their own picture that represents the stories and words on each sheet and that expresses their own love for the gospel.

After the children have drawn their pictures, sing the entire song again, letting the children use their own books as music prompts.

If time allows, invite children to come to the front and hold up the pictures that they used for a verse of the song while the song is sung a final time.

Close with your testimony of the scriptures and the messages they contain that can lead us to a greater testimony of the Savior. Encourage the children to read the scriptures and record their own testimonies as they grow.

Illustrations and Scripture References

Verse 1—*GAK* no. 212 "Sermon on the Mount." Matthew 4:23–24; Matthew 5–7; 3 Nephi 12

Verse 2—*GAK* no. 322 "Blessing the Children." 3 Nephi 17:11–24; Mark 10:13–16

Verse 3—*GAK* no. 214 "Calming the Sea." Luke 8:22–25

Tell me the stories
of Jesus I Love to hear.

Scenes by the wayside,
tales of the sea,

Oh, let me hear how the
children stood round his knee

Things I would ask him to
tell me if He were here.

Stories of Jesus,
tell them to me.

I shall imagine his
blessings resting on me;

Words full of kindness,
deeds full of grace,

Tell me, in accents of
wonder, how rolled the sea,

And how the Master,
ready and kind,

All in the love-light
of Jesus' face.

Tossing the boat in a
tempest on Galilee!

Chided the billows
and hushed the wind.

4. super scripture search

Opening Song: "Search, Ponder, and Pray," *Children's Songbook*, 109
Closing Song: "Seek the Lord Early," *Children's Songbook*, 108

Lesson Purpose

"The Doctrine and Covenants teaches me how to live the gospel" (*2008 Outline for Sharing Time and the Children's Sacrament Meeting Presentation*, 4).

Materials Needed

- Copies, one set for junior primary and one set for senior primary, of the illustrations from this lesson
- The Book of Mormon
- The Doctrine and Covenants
- Chalkboard or other display area
- Marker
- Tape or other fastener

Preparation

- Join the pieces of the large illustration together and fasten with tape or other fastener.
- Display the illustration on a flat surface at the front of the Primary room.
- Cut apart the symbol and scripture references for ease in use.

Teaching Suggestions

Ask the children to name off all the books of scripture that we have in The Church of Jesus Christ of Latter-day Saints. Testify that the scriptures contain the direction that we need to understand how to live the gospel and return to Heavenly Father. Explain that each book of scripture contains messages from Heavenly Father to His prophets from different times and places.

The Doctrine and Covenants contains messages written by modern-day prophets. Share your own testimony of the Doctrine and Covenants with the children.

Read 2 Nephi 4:15 with the children, and discuss the importance of reading and pondering the scriptures. Tell the children that today you will be helping them search the scriptures, particularly the Doctrine and Covenants, for information about what Heavenly Father would like them to try to do to live the gospel and to be happy. They will also search your picture for hidden symbols representing the things you will be discussing.

Read each scripture, and discuss the gospel concept it outlines. Invite a reverent child to come forward and search for the correct symbol in the large picture. Have the child circle the symbol with a marker. They may receive help and prompts from the rest of the children as needed. After each symbol is found, sing the corresponding song, and move on to the next scripture.

Close by re-emphasizing the importance of reading and searching the scriptures so we can stay close to Heavenly Father. As we study and search His commandments, we can find ways to bring joy into our lives through the gospel.

5. If the Savior Stood Beside Me

Sally DeFord, "If the Savior Stood Beside Me," *Friend,* Oct. 1993, 14

Opening Song: "Do As I'm Doing," *Children's Songbook,* 276
Closing Song: Sally DeFord, "If the Savior Stood Beside Me," *Friend,* Oct. 1993, 14

Lesson Purpose

"Jesus Christ showed me how to do the will of Heavenly Father" (*2008 Outline for Sharing Time and the Children's Sacrament Meeting Presentation,* 4).

Materials Needed

- Copies, on cardstock, of the illustrations from this lesson
- 9 craft sticks
- Craft knife
- Flashlight
- Flat, light-colored display area (A white sheet over the chalkboard works well.)
- Glue
- Scissors
- Table or display platform
- Tape or other fastener

Preparation

- Cut out each illustration including white areas within the illustrations. Using a craft knife will ease the difficulty of cutting small areas.
- Glue each illustration to a craft stick to be used as a handle.
- If needed, drape the sheet over your display area and secure it so that the surface is smooth.
- Place and secure the flashlight on the table, so that its light will shine on the sheet.

Teaching Suggestions

After singing "Do As I'm Doing," express how fun it is to try imitating other people. Sometimes it's fun to stand in front of a mirror and make the "other you" do silly things. Let the children stand quietly at their chair and try to mirror a few simple movements that you make.

Tell the children that there is something that follows them wherever they go and mimics their every action. Sometimes it can be seen, and sometimes it can't. Sometimes even if it can be seen, we don't notice it. Ask the children if they can guess what you are talking about.

Turn on your flashlight and place your hand in front of it so that a shadow forms on the sheet. Move your hand around, and show the children that your shadow does exactly what you do. Explain that a shadow is made when light shines on an object. Because we have been given the light of the gospel, we have also been given some special types of "shadows." These shadows are available to us as long as we are living the gospel, or standing in the light. Sometimes they are there, and we don't even notice them. When we forget about these types of shadows, we can make wrong choices.

The Holy Ghost can be our constant companion, just like a shadow. He can gently help us do what is right. The Savior eagerly watches to see if we will notice our shadow and follow His example.

Ask the children to think about what it would be like if the Savior was their shadow and was with them everywhere they went. While it is fun to make silly faces in a mirror or imitate fun actions, how would our actions change if it were the Savior standing in front of us? Could we learn to let Him choose what we should do and be like, instead trying to find our way on our own?

Testify that Jesus Christ is our ultimate example, that He will always show us what we should do if we want to be happy and return to Heavenly Father. Tell the children that a good reminder to try and choose the right is to think about the Savior standing next to us, or being our shadow, as we go about our lives every day. Thinking of Him as if He were right beside us, helps us remember to act in a way that would make Him proud.

Introduce the song at this point. Share and help the children learn each phrase, using the shadow visual aids to help in prompting. As each phrase is learned, be sure that the children understand the meaning behind their words. Introduce the melody and try singing the first verse. Invite reverent children to come up and hold the shadow prompts as they are needed for each phrase.

Repeat the learning process for the other two verses. Stop occasionally to review what has already been learned, and let other children hold the shadow prompts.

Praise their efforts to learn from the shadows that you have shown them. Remind them that the Savior loves them and has given them a beautiful example to follow. Using the words from the song as a template, ask the children to share some of the things Jesus Christ has shown us we should do.

Close by encouraging them to try to remember the Savior and invite Him to be their "shadow" during the coming week.

shadow symbols and corresponding words

Verse 1
- Savior—"If the Savior stood beside me, would I do the things I do?"
- Commandments—"Would I think of His commandments and try harder to be true?"
- Follow (people walking)—"Would I follow His example? Would I live more righteously"
- See (eye)—"If I could see the Savior standing nigh, watching over me?"

Verse 2
- Savior—"If the Savior stood beside me, would I say the things I say?"
- Words (mouth)—"Would my words be true and kind if He were never far away?"
- Share the gospel (hand with book):—"Would I try to share the gospel? Would I speak more rev'rently"
- See (eye)—"If I could see the Savior standing nigh, watching over me?"

Verse 3
- Near—"He is always near me though I do not see Him there,"
- Loves (heart)—"And be cause He loves me dearly, I am in His watchful care."
- Kind of person (CTR shield)—"So I'll be the kind of person that I know I'd like to be"
- Savior—"if I could see the Savior standing nigh, watching over me."

6. Understanding the Atonement

Opening Song: "Beautiful Savior (Crusader's Hymn)," *Children's Songbook*, 62
Closing Song: Sally DeFord, "If the Savior Stood Beside Me," *Friend*, Oct. 1993, 14

Lesson Purpose

"Jesus Christ loves me. Because of His Atonement, I can repent and live with Heavenly Father again" (*2008 Outline for Sharing Time and the Children's Sacrament Meeting Presentation, 4*).

Materials Needed

- Copies of the scripture reference pages from this lesson
- *GAK* no. 227
- The scriptures
- 2 small Easter baskets
- 7 plastic Easter eggs
- Marker
- Paper
- Scissors

Preparation

- Cut apart the scripture references.
- Provide your pianist with a list of the songs.
- Become familiar with each of the noted scriptures.
- Place a strip inside each Easter egg and write the corresponding number on the outside.
- Place all the eggs inside one basket.

Teaching Suggestions

Begin by showing the children the picture of Christ. Share your own brief testimony of the Savior with the children. Remind them that even though we can choose some fun ways to celebrate Easter, we need to remember that Christ is the true reason for our happiness. Ask the children if they can tell you what special event we are showing thankfulness for when we celebrate Easter. Commend them for their answers and reinforce the value of Christ's gifts of the Atonement and Resurrection.

Show the children the basket of eggs. Tell them that they will help you find the true meaning of Easter as they help you find these eggs. Each egg contains a scripture that will tell them more about the Atonement.

Invite two reverent children to come to the front of the room. One child will go into the hallway while the other child hides the first egg in the Primary room.

When the egg has been hidden, invite the first child back into the room. He will search for the egg by listening to the rest of the children sing the corresponding song. They will sing louder when he is close to the egg and softer when he is farther away. If the child is having difficulty finding the egg, have the children repeat the song, or continue on to the next verse as appropriate, while you help the child find the egg.

Always finish the song, even after the egg is found. This allows the children to refocus on the music and its message.

Open the egg, and have the children look up the scripture and read it with you. Discuss its meaning and clarify any questions that the children might have before going to the next egg.

Place the eggs that have been opened into the other basket so they don't get mixed in with the unopened ones.

Close by showing the picture of the Savior again and by re-emphasizing your testimony. Be mindful of the Spirit, and help the children understand its presence as you speak.

scripture references for easter eggs

2 Nephi 2:21—We came to this earth to be tested. Heavenly Father knew we would make mistakes.

1 Nephi 15:34–35—Our mistakes make us less like Heavenly Father. They keep us from being able to be with Him again when we die.

2 Nephi 9:23—We have the gift of the Atonement to help us become clean again. We learn to have faith in Jesus Christ and His Atonement when we repent.

D&C 19:16—Jesus Christ suffered for all of our sins and sorrows, to open a way for us to return to Heavenly Father.

Isaiah 1:18—Through the Atonement, Christ can take away all of our sins. If we repent, we can be clean again.

D&C 58:42 —When we show that we are sorry and have truly repented, we can be forgiven.

Ether 12:27—Heavenly Father helps us learn and be better every time we repent.

scripture references and songs

2 Nephi 2:21—"I Will Follow God's Plan," *Children's Songbook,* 164

1 Nephi 15:34—"I Lived in Heaven," *Children's Songbook,* 4

2 Nephi 9:23—"He Sent His Son," *Children's Songbook,* 34

D&C 19:16—"The Third Article of Faith," *Children's Songbook,* 123

Isaiah 1:18—"When I Am Baptized," *Children's Songbook,* 103

D&C 58:42—"Help Me, Dear Father," *Children's Songbook,* 99

Ether 12:27—"Nephi's Courage," *Children's Songbook,* 120

7. We Thank Thee, O God, for a Prophet

Hymns, no. 19

Opening Song: "Follow the Prophet," *Children's Songbook,* 110
Closing Song: "We Thank Thee, O God, for a Prophet," *Hymns,* no. 19

Lesson Purpose

"The prophet holds all priesthood keys and leads the Church as directed by the Lord" (*2008 Outline for Sharing Time and the Children's Sacrament Meeting Presentation,* 5).

Materials Needed

- *GAK* no. 520
- The Holy Bible
- Blank paper
- Crayons or colored pencils

Preparation

- This lesson focuses on teaching all of the children the first verse only. If desired, consider inviting the achievement girls and cub scouts to each learn one of the other verses as part of their activities.

Teaching Suggestions

Show the children your picture of President Hinckley. Ask the children who he is and what makes him special. He is the prophet and president of the Church. We follow him because Heavenly Father has given him special gifts and abilities in order to lead us. These special gifts have to do with the priesthood, or a righteous man's ability to act in the name of God. Testify that President Hinckley holds all the priesthood keys that can be given to a righteous priesthood holder. Heavenly Father trusts President Hinckley to use those keys to lead us righteously and help us know how to return to Him. Review Amos 3:7 with the children.

Hold the picture of the prophet in front of you and ask the children to quietly form a line behind you. Challenge them to reverently follow the "prophet" as he leads them around the room in a short game of "follow the leader." After they have returned to their seats, help the children understand that President Hinckley tries his best to help us know how much Heavenly Father and Jesus Christ love us and help us do things that will help us return to live with them again. That is why it is important for us to try our best to listen to what the prophet says and do what he asks us to.

Express gratitude for the living prophet.

Today the children will begin learning a hymn to help them remember to be grateful for the prophet and try their hardest to follow him.

Divide the children into four groups with an adult in each group. Assign each group one sentence from the first verse of "We Thank Thee, O God, for a Prophet." Have the adults help the children talk about and understand what the wording of their sentence and discuss a way that they can illustration this message on their paper. As they draw and discuss have the adult help them repeat the words of their sentence until they are familiar with it.

After the groups have finished their individual work, invite the groups up in order of the song to present their sentence. They will show their illustration and tell the other children what they have learned about their message.

Next introduce the melody to the song. Help the children identify where their sentence fits within the song. Have one reverent child from each group come forward to hold up their group's picture when it is their turn to sing. Help the children practice singing along with the piano only for the portion of the song they learned with their group. Practice this several times until the song proceeds smoothly. Commend the children for their efforts in following along and helping each other sing the song.

Next, ask the children to begin combining their efforts even further. Those children who have the first two sentences will begin working together to sing these sentences as a whole instead of separately. The children with the last two sentences will also combine. Sing the song again in this manner several times.

By this point in time, the children will have had a great deal of exposure to all of the words. Go back to the illustrations the children created and walk all the children through the words and a brief summary of the message, then challenge them to try and sing the entire song from beginning to end. Reverent children can again be used to hold the drawn prompts and encourage the children to sing.

Tell the children that the manner in which they learned this song is similar to holding the keys of the priesthood. A worthy young man receives the keys of Aaronic priesthood when he turns twelve. If he stays worthy, he works with and learns from other worthy priesthood holders. As he grows he may hold more keys, including the Melchizedek priesthood, according to what the Lord needs him to do. Remind the children that the prophet is the only one on earth who holds all of the priesthood keys (or the whole song) and helps people learn and grow from them.

Close with your gratitude for a living prophet and the children's enthusiasm to learn to follow him.

8. The Value of the Book of Mormon

Opening Song: "Keep the Commandments," *Children's Songbook*, 146
Closing Song: "Stand for the Right," *Children's Songbook*, 159

Lesson Purpose

"The prophet teaches me to read and pray about the Book of Mormon" (*2008 Outline for Sharing Time and the Children's Sacrament Meeting Presentation*, 5).

Materials Needed

- Church Distribution Item no. 54116000: Church History Collection (DVD)
- Copies of the *Children's Songbook*
- *GAK* no. 520 and the Book of Mormon section of the *GAK*
- Television and DVD player

Preparation

- Prepare the DVD to show the section "Parley P. Pratt Finds the Book of Mormon" (13:25).
- Prayerfully consider any challenges you would like to extend to your Primary children regarding the Book of Mormon.

Teaching Suggestions

Begin by showing the prepared video portion. At its conclusion, talk about what makes the Book of Mormon special. Share a brief testimony of the Book of Mormon and what makes it special to you.

Divide the children into their classes. Have each class choose a *GAK* picture that represents their favorite Book of Mormon story to share with the rest of the children. They should also choose a corresponding song.

Classes will then share their pictures and stories with the rest of the children. Sing each chosen song before moving to the next group.

At the conclusion, remind the children of President Benson's challenge to read the Book of Mormon. Tell the children that the prophets continue to share a strong testimony of the Book of Mormon and still extend the challenge to read the Book of Mormon and gain our own testimony of its truthfulness.

Close with the picture of President Hinckley and his challenges and promises concerning reading the Book of Mormon, which are included in this lesson. Issue any challenges you wish to extend to your Primary children.

President Hinckley's Quotes about the Book of Mormon

"Believe in the Book of Mormon as another witness of the Son of God. This book has come forth as an added testimony to the world of the great truths concerning the Master as set forth in the Bible. The Bible is the testament of the Old World. The Book of Mormon is the testament of the New World, and they go hand in hand in testimony of the Lord Jesus Christ. I can't understand why those of other faiths cannot accept the Book of Mormon. One would think that they would be looking for additional witnesses to the great and solemn truths of the Bible. We have that witness, my brothers and sisters, this marvelous book of inspiration which affirms the validity and the truth of the divine nature of the Son of God. God be thanked for this precious and wonderful testimony. Let us read it. Let us dwell upon its truths. Let us learn its message and be blessed accordingly." (Gordon B. Hinckley, Address delivered in Baltimore, Maryland, 15 Nov. 1998)

"Very near the end of its 239 chapters, you will find a challenge issued by the prophet Moroni as he completed his record nearly sixteen centuries ago. Said he: 'And I exhort you to remember these things; for the time speedily cometh that ye shall know that I lie not, for ye shall see me at the bar of God; and the Lord God will say unto you: Did I not declare my words unto you, which were written by this man, like as one crying from the dead, yea, even as one speaking out of the dust? . . . And God shall show unto you, that that which I have written is true' (Moroni 10:27, 29). Without reservation I promise you that if each of you will [read the Book of Mormon], there will come into your lives and into your homes an added measure of the Spirit of the Lord, a strengthened resolution to walk in obedience to His commandments, and a stronger testimony of the living reality of the Son of God." (Gordon B. Hinckley, "A Testimony Vibrant and True," *Ensign,* Aug. 2005, 2–6)

9. home

Children's Songbook, 192

Opening Song: "Love Is Spoken Here," *Children's Songbook,* 190
Closing Song: "Home," *Children's Songbook,* 192

Lesson Purpose

"Each member of my family has a divine role" (*2008 Outline for Sharing Time and the Children's Sacrament Meeting Presentation,* 5).

Materials Needed

- "The Family: A Proclamation to the World," *Ensign,* Nov. 1995, 102
- Dress-up clothing for each member of a family (mother, father, and child)

Teaching Suggestions

Talk about what comes to the children's minds when you say the word "home." What kinds of memories and feelings does it represent to the children? Testify that Heavenly Father gave each of us a special family that could help us learn and grow into who He needed us to be.

Share the first verse of the song with the children. Allow them to repeat the words several times and hear the melody before trying to sing the verse.

Show the family proclamation to the children. Share its role in helping define what Heavenly Father would like our families to be like. Emphasize that each person in a family has a divine role and mission, a special part to play in helping the family be happy and eternal.

Ask the children to list the roles of the family that they can think of (mother, father, and child).

Show the children the dress-up clothing. Begin with father. Have a reverent child come to the front and dress in the father's clothing. The children must identify special things that a father can do in a family. For each thing that they are able to identify, the "father" will put on one article of clothing.

When the child has dressed completely, testify of the important role of fathers and share the phrase about fathers from the second verse of the song. Have the children repeat it and try to sing just this phrase as the "father" removes his dress-up clothing.

Repeat this same process for mother and child. When all the words have been learned, sing the second verse as a whole.

Follow this with a reminder that Heavenly Father has a plan for us; He provides guidance and direction, such as the family proclamation, to help us have happy homes. Teach the third verse of the song to the children. After the children have had a chance to practice this verse, remind them of the order and messages of the first and second verses as well.

Call six reverent children up to represent the messages as you sing all three verses. The first child will hold his arms over his head like a roof. ("Home is where the heart is and warmth and love abound.") The second child will give herself a hug. ("Home is warm, circling arms go all the way around.") The next three children will choose one article of dress-up clothing to represent the members of the family. The sixth child will hold the family proclamation for the third verse.

If time remains, choose another set of children to act out the prompts as the children practice the song again.

Close with your testimony of the divine nature of families and the important roles Heavenly Father has given each of its members.

10. establish a house

Opening Song: "The Wise Man and the Foolish Man," *Children's Songbook,* 281
Closing Song: "Home," *Children's Songbook,* 192

Lesson Purpose

"Scripture study, family prayer, and family home evening can strengthen my family" (*2008 Outline for Sharing Time and the Children's Sacrament Meeting Presentation,* 5).

materials needed

- Copy of the house pieces from this lesson
- The Doctrine and Covenants
- The Holy Bible
- Chalkboard or other display area
- Tape or other fastener

Preparation

- Cut apart and laminate the illustrations from this lesson.

Teaching Suggestions

Have the children read Doctrine and Covenants 88:119. Discuss what type of house this scripture can refer to. Remind them that when the Savior comes to earth, He usually comes to the temple since it is His house. This scripture tells us what types of things should be present in His house.

Read and discuss the following passage from the bible dictionary: "A temple is literally a house of the Lord. . . . A place where the Lord may come, it is the most holy of any place of worship on the earth. Only the home can compare with the temple in sacredness" (Bible Dictionary, "Temple," 780).

If we can do the things listed in Doctrine and Covenants 88:119 in our own homes, the Spirit can be there with us, and Jesus will know He is welcome there. Ask the children for their ideas about what they can do in their own families to make them happier and more centered on the gospel.

Testify of the need to build strong families focused on the Savior and His teachings. Show the children the pieces to the house that you would like to build for your family. Each piece represents an important building block that will help to keep a family strong and happy.

Have children pick pieces of the house; discuss what the building block is and how it can become a part of their homes. Sing a related song for each piece. As the children pick a piece, assemble the home on a chalkboard or other display area.

Close by reinforcing the sacred nature of our homes and encouraging the children to always be on the lookout for things they can do help their homes stay on the firm foundation of the gospel.

suggested songs

Faith—"I Am a Child of God," *Children's Songbook,* 2

Family Home Evening—"Family Night," *Children's Songbook,* 195

Love—"Home," *Children's Songbook,* 192

Peace— Sally DeFord, "If the Savior Stood Beside Me," *Friend,* Oct. 1993, 14

Prayer—"Family Prayer," *Children's Songbook,* 189

Scripture Study—"Tell Me the Stories of Jesus," *Children's Songbook,* 157

Work—"When We're Helping," *Children's Songbook,* 198

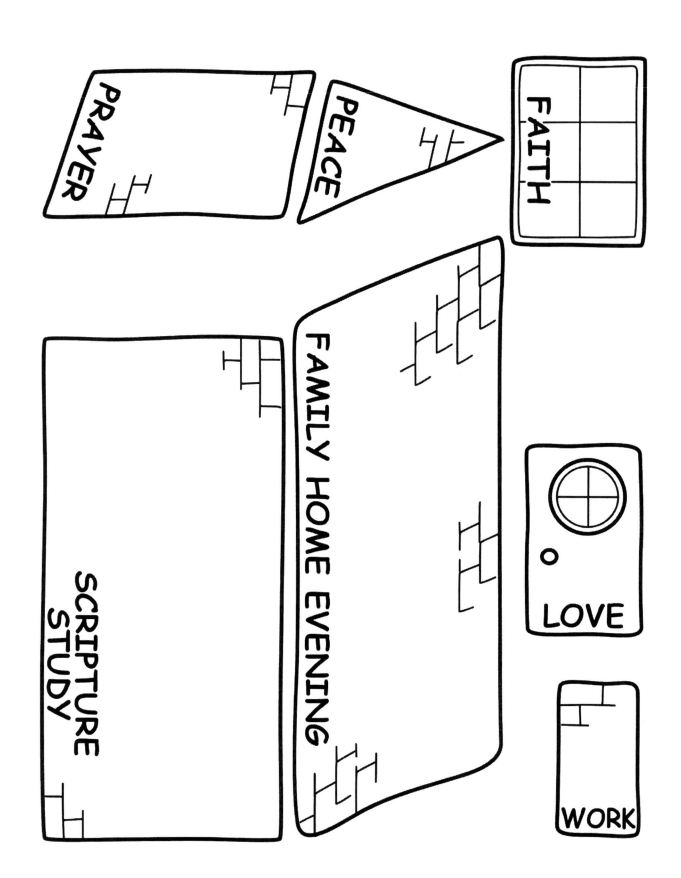

11. I Love to See the Temple

Children's Songbook, 95

Opening Song: "Families Can Be Together Forever," *Children's Songbook,* 188
Closing Song: "I Love to See the Temple," *Children's Songbook,* 95

Lesson Purpose

"I will live now to be worthy to go to the temple and do my part to have an eternal family" (*2008 Outline for Sharing Time and the Children's Sacrament Meeting Presentation,* 6).

Materials Needed

- Copies of the illustrations from this lesson (Make three copies of the footprints containing the words "love" and "temple.")
- Chalkboard or other display area
- Scissors
- Tape or other fastener

Preparation

- Cut out and laminate the illustrations.
- Mount the footprints across the bottom of the chalkboard.
- Mount the picture of the temple on the upper right corner of the chalkboard.

Teaching Suggestions

Tell the children that today you are going to talk about a special place that we can go to here on earth to be close to Heavenly Father. Draw the children's attention to the picture of the temple, and discuss what makes the temple a special place. Allow the children to share what they know about the temple.

Share your own testimony of the temple. Encourage the children to work toward being able to attend the temple and to do all they can to help their families become happy, "forever" families. Emphasize a few of the important steps, such as remaining pure and clean, that people must take in order to be worthy to go to the temple.

Show the children the footprints at the bottom of the chalkboard. Help the children understand that these prints show key words from the song "I Love to See the Temple." As you share the words to the song and discuss their meaning with the children, invite reverent children to find the key words from each phrase and place them in order on a path leading to the temple. The second verse can form a second path underneath the first.

Sing each verse as it is learned, and invite a reverent child to point to the word prompts as the children sing the song as a whole.

Review the concepts discussed in the verses with the children.

Ask the children questions about the temple and the song. Children who answer correctly may choose a footprint to remove from the board. Try singing the song again after a few of the footprints have been removed.

Close with your testimony about temples and their importance.

sample questions

Why does Heavenly Father want us to go to the temple?

What does the Holy Spirit feel like?

Why is a temple holy?

What do we have to have before we can go inside a temple that has been dedicated to the Lord?

What is a covenant?

What does it mean to be sealed together as a family?

Why are families so important to Heavenly Father?

What is our closest temple?

How many temples do you think there are right now?

Whose house is a temple?

How can you start preparing now to be able to go to the temple?

love

Holy Spirit

temple

some day

prepare

beauty

House of God

pray

holy place

promise

covenant

duty

family

truth

child of God

sealed

12. Tithing Builds the Kingdom

Opening Song: "Thanks to Our Father," *Children's Songbook, 20*
Closing Song: "I Want to Give the Lord My Tenth," *Children's Songbook, 150*

Lesson Purpose

"My tithing helps to build temples" (*2008 Outline for Sharing Time and the Children's Sacrament Meeting Presentation, 6*).

Materials Needed

- Copies, on cardstock, of the illustrations from this lesson
- The scriptures
- 7 sheets of brown construction paper
- Chalkboard and chalk
- Marker
- No. 10 can or other large circle that can be traced
- Scissors
- Tape or other fastener

Preparation

- Trace the bottom of the no. 10 can onto each piece of brown construction paper.
- Cut out the circles.
- Draw a dollar sign on one side of each circle.
- List the questions outlined in this lesson on the other side your circles.
- Write "tithing" on the top of your chalkboard, and place your penny circles—dollar sign up—on the left side of the board.
- Cut the picture of the temple into the seven marked puzzle pieces, and set them aside face down.

Teaching Suggestions

Introduce the subject of tithing, and allow the children to share a few things they know about tithing. Commend them for their answers. Remind the children that sometimes the tithing that we pay can seem like a very little thing, but when everyone does their part, the little pieces can add up to something great. Tell the children that as they learn more about tithing, they will put together a picture of one of the great things that paying our tithing can do.

Invite a reverent child to come forward and turn over one of your paper coins. Read the question to the children, and ask them to share their answers with you. You may choose to write a few of their answers on the board beside the appropriate coin.

Next, have the children look up the scripture answer to each question and read it with you. Reinforce the scripture and concept with the children before singing the corresponding song.

After the song, invite a reverent child to choose a piece of your puzzle to post on the board. When the puzzle is complete and all the questions have been answered, briefly review the things that you have covered with the children. Then, close the lesson with your own testimony of tithing and of its importance in building temples and churches and helping the members of the Church. Encourage the children to pay an honest tithing so that they can be worthy to go to the temple and receive special blessings from Heavenly Father.

Questions, Scripture References, and Songs

1. Do we get blessings from paying our tithing? (Malachi 3:10)

   If we pay our tithing, Heavenly Father will give us even more blessings.

   "I'm Glad to Pay a Tithing," *Children's Songbook,* 150.

2. Should it make us happy or sad to pay tithing? (2 Corinthians 9:7)

   Tithing is a way we can show gratitude for the blessings Heavenly Father gives us.

   "Smiles," *Children's Songbook,* 267

3. What can tithing be used for? (D&C 97:12)

   Tithing money usually pays for things like the welfare program, building and maintaining temples and church buildings, and sometimes even education needs. It also supports missionaries and family history programs.

   "When I Go to Church," *Children's Songbook,* 157

4. Is tithing a commandment? (D&C 119:4)

   Paying tithing is a test of faith and a commandment.

   "Keep the Commandments," *Children's Songbook,* 146

5. How much should we pay as tithing? (Genesis 28:22)

   Tithing is ten percent of all your income. Show the children how to "hop" the decimal point to the left one number place to make 10 percent and figure out the amount of their tithing for any amount of money.

   "I Want to Give the Lord My Tenth," *Children's Songbook,* 150

6. Who do we give our tithing to? (D&C 119:1)

   We pay our tithing to our bishop or branch president. They send the money to the headquarters of the church. The First Presidency, the Quorum of the Twelve Apostles, and the Presiding Bishopric prayerfully determine where the money should be used.

   "Our Bishop," *Children's Songbook,* 135

7. Do we have to pay tithing to go to the temple? (D&C 119:5)

   Paying a full tithing is a requirement for getting a temple recommend.

   "I Love to See the Temple," *Children's Songbook,* 95

13. Called to serve

Children's Songbook, 174–75

Opening Song: "We'll Bring the World His Truth (Army of Helaman)," *Children's Songbook,* 172
Closing Song: "Called to Serve," *Children's Songbook,* 174–75

Lesson Purpose

"I will prepare to be a missionary by being faithful and obedient" (*2008 Outline for Sharing Time and the Children's Sacrament Meeting Presentation,* 7).

Preparation

• Prior to the day of this lesson, invite a set of missionaries to come in and participate in teaching the children this message and song.

Teaching suggestions

Ask the children to briefly share what they know about missionaries. Who do they know that has served a mission, where did they go, and what do the children think those people did on their missions?

Help the children understand that young people and older couples go on missions because they love Heavenly Father and the gospel. They love other people and want them to be able to learn about the gospel as well. Encourage the children to plan for and look forward to the time when they can show their love for Heavenly Father and share their testimony by going on a mission.

Introduce the chorus of the song first. Let the children hear the piano play the chorus and help them clap along to the beat of the music. Prompt them to imagine that they are missionaries marching out to find people to teach the gospel to.

Next, share the words, letting the children continue to clap along with the rhythm. After they are somewhat familiar with the words, ask them to count how many times they sing the words "onward" and "forward" as they sing along with the piano (seven).

Allow the children to form an army-style marching line and march forward one step every time they sing the words "onward" or "forward." Have the children turn around and march back as they sing the chorus one more time. Then ask the children to return to their seats.

Introduce the missionaries. They will teach the words in each verse to the children by sharing them in short phrases and briefly explaining how they accomplish the things the song talks about as missionaries. After the missionaries have taught and reviewed the words to the first verse with the children, have the children stand at their seats and sing the verse with the chorus, marching in place at the key words in the chorus. The missionaries should teach the second verse in the same manner.

After the children have learned all the verses, sing the entire song again, and let the missionaries close by sharing a brief testimony with the children and by challenging the children to live the gospel faithfully so that they too can serve missions.

14. Be a Missionary Now

Opening Song: "Called to Serve," *Children's Songbook, 174–75*
Closing Song: "The Things I Do," *Children's Songbook, 170*

Lesson Purpose

"I help to bless others when I share the gospel" (*2008 Outline for Sharing Time and the Children's Sacrament Meeting Presentation, 7*).

Materials Needed

- Copies, on cardstock, of the illustrations from this lesson (Make five copies of the fish illustration, and situate one quote from this lesson to the back of each fish.)
- *GAK* no. 209
- The Holy Bible
- 20 large paper clips
- Basket for the "caught" fish
- Doughnut-shaped magnet (available at craft and education stores)
- Paint-stirring stick
- Scissors
- Small wading pool or blue bed sheet to represent water
- Yarn or string (measuring 2 feet)

Preparation

- Color and cut out the fish illustrations from this lesson.
- Laminate the fish for durability.
- Place a paper clip over the mouth of each fish.
- Tie one end of the string to the end of the paint stick.
- Tie the other end of the string around the magnet.
- Place the wading pool on the floor, or swirl the blue sheet into a circle that looks like water.
- Scatter the fish randomly, face up, in the empty wading pool or on the blue sheet.

Teaching Suggestions

Show the children the *GAK* picture. Ask them to help you tell the story of the calling of the Apostles. Read Matthew 4:18–20 with the children.

Ask the children what they think the Apostles did that made them "fishers of men." Allow them to share their answers. Help the children understand that Jesus Christ has asked each of us to do the same things that the Apostles did. He has asked us to follow Him and be fishers of men. Each of us has been called to share the gospel no matter how old we are, where we live, or anything else. Bear your testimony of the importance of missionary work, and help the children understand that there are things they can do everyday to be missionaries. Ask the children to share a few suggestions they might have for how they can share the gospel.

Show the children your "pond," and explain that they will get to go fishing for ideas about how to be fishers of men. Invite reverent children to come to the front and use the magnetic fishing pole to choose a fish from the pond. After each fish is caught, place it in the basket.

Sing the songs as they are chosen, and briefly discuss their messages.

Read and allow the children to expand on the ideas listed on the fish.

Close with your testimony of encouragement that as the children look for ways to share the gospel and become fishers of men. Heavenly Father will help and bless them.

I Want
to Be a
Missionary Now
#168

I Hope
They Call Me
on a Mission
#169

Called
to Serve
#174

The Things I Do
#170

He Sent
His Son
#34

The
Church of
Jesus Christ
#77

A Young
Man Prepared
#166

We'll
Bring the
World His
Truth
#172

Wear
a CTR
Ring

Search,
Ponder,
and Pray
#109

Read
the Book
of Mormon in
public

Seek
the Lord
Early
#108

Invite
non-members
to your
baptism

Teach
a friend
a primary
song

Don't
be afraid
to make good
choices

Watch
a church
movie with
a friend

Hang a
picture of
Christ in your
room

Ask
a friend
about their
church

Invite
a friend to
Family Home
Evening

Invite
a friend to
a church
Activity

15. When Jesus Christ was Baptized

Children's Songbook, 102

Opening Song: "I Like My Birthdays," *Children's Songbook,* 104
Closing Song: "When Jesus Christ Was Baptized," *Children's Songbook,* 102

Lesson Purpose

"I will show my faith by being baptized and confirmed and keeping my baptismal covenants" (*2008 Outline for Sharing Time and the Children's Sacrament Meeting Presentation,* 7).

Materials Needed

- Copy of the illustration from this lesson
- *GAK* no. 208 and 601
- Chalkboard and chalk
- Tape or other fastener

Preparation

- Draw a vertical line down the middle of the chalkboard, dividing it half.

Teaching Suggestions

Show the children the picture of Jesus Christ being baptized. Help the children discuss what is happening in the picture and its importance.

Next, show the picture of the modern-day baptism. Let the children draw comparisons between the two scenes, and talk about why it is important for each of us to be baptized.

Place the picture of Jesus at the top of the left side of the chalkboard. Place the other baptism picture at the top of the right side.

Explain to the children that they will be learning a song about these two scenes. It will help them remember the importance of baptism. They will assist you with learning this song by helping create illustrations to represent the words they will learn.

Ask the children to listen carefully as you repeat the words of the first verse for them. Have them tell you which picture the verse talks about and what key words they remember you saying. Commend them for their responses.

Begin teaching the song phrase by phrase. Place the included illustration of Jesus in the middle of the left side of the chalkboard for the phrase "When Jesus Christ was baptized." Repeat the phrase with the children, and build upon it as they draw new elements of the picture: the river, the number three, a heart, words from heaven, and a dove.

Be sure the children understand that the Holy Ghost is not actually a dove. This is just a symbol that is sometimes used to help us understand that the Spirit is gentle, soft, and quiet and that it can bring us peace.

After the children have drawn their description of the verse, repeat the words again, pointing to the appropriate symbols they drew. Then have the children try singing the entire verse.

Next, focus the children's attention on the other *GAK* picture. Ask them what they think the second verse of the song will talk about. Remind them of the things they discussed about the importance of baptism. Then let the children illustrate this verse on the right side of the board. Illustrations would include a child, a priesthood holder, the water, a church building, and the dove (to again represent the Holy Ghost). As you draw and teach the wording, be sure to discuss the sacred nature of this ordinance and help the children understand the words and information portrayed.

Sing the second verse as a whole, and combine the two verses.

Continue practicing by asking the children questions about baptism. Children giving the correct answers should be invited to the front to choose a verse to sing while the they point to the picture prompts drawn on the board.

Close with your testimony of baptism and of the covenants we make with Heavenly Father when we are baptized.

16. Remembering Jesus from Head to Toe

Opening Song: "Before I Take the Sacrament," *Children's Songbook, 73*
Closing Song: "To Think about Jesus," *Children's Songbook, 71*

Lesson Purpose

"When I take the sacrament, I renew my baptismal covenants" (*2008 Outline for Sharing Time and the Children's Sacrament Meeting Presentation, 7*).

Materials Needed

- Copies of the illustration and word strips from this lesson
- *GAK* no. 225, 601, and 604
- The Book of Mormon
- The Doctrine and Covenants
- Chalkboard or other display area
- Scissors
- Tape or other fastener

Preparation

- Post the man illustration on the chalkboard.
- Cut apart the word strips.

Teaching Suggestions

Show the children the three *GAK* pictures. Ask them what the pictures have in common. Help the children understand that during the last supper Jesus Christ gave us the ordinance of the sacrament as a way to remember what He would sacrifice for us.

Read Mosiah 18:8–10 with the children, and discuss the concepts listed. Help them understand the meaning behind the scripture. When we are baptized, we make special promises to Heavenly Father and to Jesus Christ, including a promise to always remember Jesus and to try to be like Him. When we take the sacrament, we are given a chance to remember our promises, to correct our mistakes, and to find ways to be better people. Read D&C 20:77 with the children. Help the children recognize that this is the prayer said for the bread every week in the sacrament ordinance. Emphasize that the time during the sacrament is special and sacred. It is a quiet and thoughtful time to remember Jesus Christ.

Encourage the children by explaining that even though it is sometimes hard, they can learn to quiet their bodies and minds while they think about Jesus during this special time. Show the picture of baptism and emphasize the process of immersion that cleanses our whole bodies and commits us from head to toe to follow Jesus Christ and carry His name. Today's lesson will help the children practice quieting their body, letting it help them remember Jesus Christ and the promises we have made to Him.

Refer the children to the man illustration. Start with the head, and talk about ways that you can keep your head quiet. Post the appropriate word strip by the head, and relate how it can help in remembering the Savior during the sacrament. Sing the accompanying song before moving on to the next body part. Continue this process with the rest of the word strips.

Close with your testimony of the Savior and the sacred renewal time of the sacrament. Reinforce your encouragement that the children can quiet their bodies as they think about Jesus from head to toe during the administration of sacrament.

Word Strip Placement and Meanings

Head—Agency. Heavenly Father gave us agency so that we could make choices. He knew sometimes we would make the wrong choice, so He sent the Savior to help us correct our mistakes.

Sing: "I Will Follow God's Plan," *Children's Songbook,* 164

Shoulders—Trials. Everyone will have problems they have to work out during their lives. There are things that can seem very difficult and can make us sad and discouraged. Jesus Christ understands these problems and how they make us feel. He can help us be stronger and find our way through our trials.

Sing: "Heavenly Father, Now I Pray," *Children's Songbook,* 19

Arms—Work. We promise Heavenly Father that we will try our best to do what is right when we are baptized. We also promise to help each other and to serve those around us.

Sing: "I Will Be Valiant," *Children's Songbook,* 162

Hands—Scriptures. We turn to the scriptures to learn about Jesus Christ. They tell us about His life and His Atonement. They tell us how to be like Him.

Sing: "Tell Me the Stories of Jesus," *Children's Songbook,* 57

Chest—Heart. Our hearts can feel the presence of the Holy Ghost. It is the gift we are given at baptism. When we are worthy it will guide us and help us to remember the Savior. When we do something wrong, He can help us know that we need to repent.

Sing: "Help Me, Dear Father," *Children's Songbook,* 99

Knees—Prayers. We talk to Heavenly Father and Jesus Christ in our prayers. We can be close to Them. We can ask for help and forgiveness. We can express gratitude for the Atonement.

Sing: "A Child's Prayer," *Children's Songbook,* 12

Legs—Witness. When we are baptized we promise to always stand as a witness of Jesus Christ, to be an example of the things He wants us to be. We are proud to stand up and share His gospel and name with those around us.

Sing: "Called to Serve," *Children's Songbook,* 174–75

Feet—Example. We need to follow Christ's example, stay close to the Spirit, and walk only on paths that Jesus would want us to walk. When we find ourselves where we shouldn't be, we need to remember the Savior's example, turn around and go back to where He is.

Sing: Sally DeFord, "If the Savior Stood Beside Me," *Friend,* Oct. 1993, 14

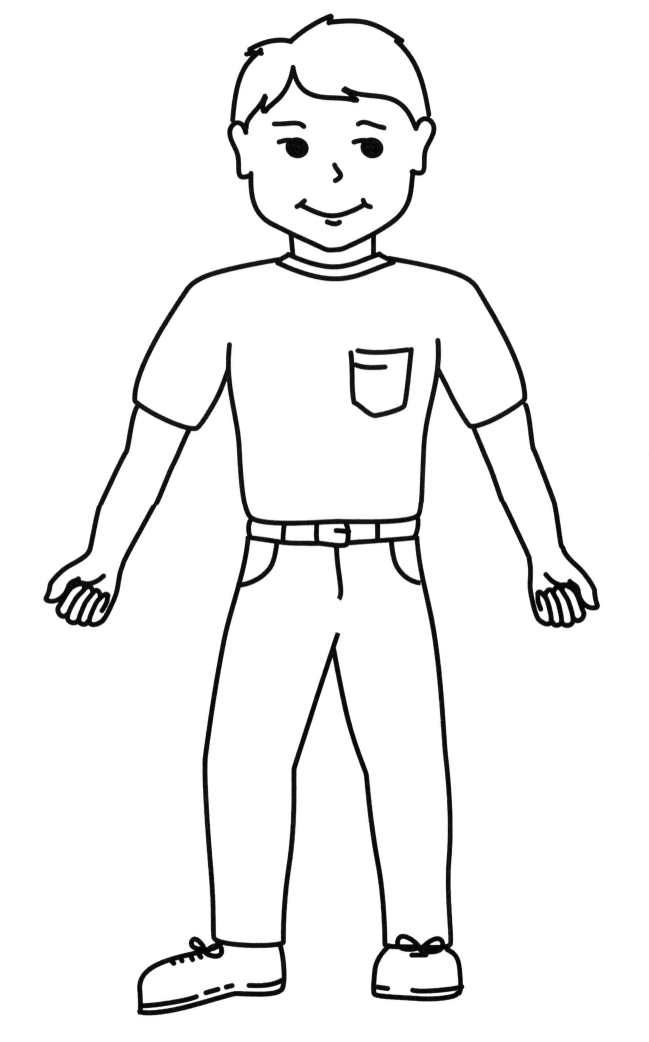

agency

trials

work

scriptures

heart

prayers

witness

example

17. I Pray in Faith

Children's Songbook, 14

Opening Song: "A Child's Prayer," *Children's Songbook,* 12
Closing Song: "I Pray in Faith," *Children's Songbook,* 14

Lesson Purpose

"I learn about prayer from the scriptures" (*2008 Outline for Sharing Time and the Children's Sacrament Meeting Presentation,* 8).

Materials Needed

- Copies of the word strips from this lesson
- *GAK* no. 403
- The Book of Mormon
- Chalkboard and chalk
- Small platform (Use a sturdy chair or low table that will support a child's weight.)

Preparation

- Become familiar with the story of the Zoramites and the Rameumptom found in Alma 31:8–23.

Teaching Suggestions

Give the children a brief overview of this story, and allow one of the children to come forward and read a verse of the prayer of the Zoramites from the top of the platform. Ask this child to share how it felt to have to stand up there and repeat that passage. They will probably respond that they felt rather silly or uncomfortable. Ask them if they felt the Spirit while they were trying to "pray" this way.

Next, show the picture of the First Vision. Have the children briefly tell you the story and compare the differences between how Joseph Smith prayed and how the Zoramites prayed. Share your testimony of the First Vision, and help the children recognize that the Spirit is now present. Emphasize that this is the same Spirit that they can feel every time they pray. Just as Heavenly Father answered Joseph Smith's sincere prayer, He will answer ours when we pray in faith.

Introduce the first verse of the song at this point. The words are straightforward and should be fairly easy to remember. Divide it into two stanzas: "I kneel to pray every day. I speak to Heavenly Father," and "He hears and answers me, when I pray in faith." Have the children repeat these words several times. Then let them hear what the music sounds like. Have the children try singing along with the melody, not the accompaniment.

Show the children your word strips, and ask them to help you put them in order as they are used in prayer. As they are placed in order, briefly discuss what the words mean. Then repeat the words of the second verse that match the word strips.

When the children can recite each set of words, add the melody line. Put the two verses together, one after the other, with only the melody line playing. Divide the children into two groups, and see if they can sing the two verses at the same time while the piano plays only the melody lines (you might want to give your pianist some prior warning so they can practice if they need to, or allow two people to play together).

If time remains, introduce the accompaniment, and let the children try singing the verses in order, then together, with the accompaniment.

This song is also beautiful a cappella. Have the piano (or perhaps a flute or violin) simply play the melody lines for the first and second times through, and then let the children sing together without instrumental accompaniment.

Open

Give Thanks

Ask

Close

18. Choosing Prayer Anytime, Anywhere

Opening Song: "I Pray in Faith," *Children's Songbook,* 14
Closing Song: "I Feel My Savior's Love," *Children's Songbook,* 74

Lesson Purpose

"Heavenly Father wants me to pray to Him often—anytime, anywhere" (*2008 Outline for Sharing Time and the Children's Sacrament Meeting Presentation,* 8).

Materials Needed

- *GAK* no. 117, 227, 305, 310, 318, 321, and 403
- The Book of Mormon
- The Holy Bible

Preparation

- Become familiar with the scripture story associated with each *GAK* picture.

Teaching Suggestions

Tell the children that during our lives we will face many different problems and many different things that can bring us happiness. Because of the gift of agency that we have been given, we each can choose how we respond to these situations. Heavenly Father doesn't leave us alone when we have a choice to make. He provides many ways for us to know how to make a good choice. Today the children will help you discuss several different situations and find one way that Heavenly Father can be a part of our lives in good times and bad.

Discuss each modern-day situation one at a time. Allow the children to voice their opinions and answers concerning what the child the story should do to solve their problem. After each scenario has been discussed, share the corresponding *GAK* picture and story of prayer from the scriptures. Commend the children for their answers and solutions, but always bring the discussion back to the need for prayer as an important step in solving each problem.

As the children begin to understand that each solution will include the step of prayer, guide their discussion to include how prayer could be useful, what that prayer might include, and what types of answers might be received.

Share Alma 33:3–11 with the children. Help them understand that this scripture reinforces the many different places and situations that we can pray in. Testify that even though the situation and answers received in the scripture stories might be slightly different from problems we encounter today, Heavenly Father wants us to understand that we can turn to Him in prayer—anytime, anywhere. When we pray, Heavenly Father always hears and answers our prayers.

Share Jeremiah 29:12–13 with the children. Help them understand that they can pray in these same places in their own lives and trust that Heavenly Father will help them.

Close by sharing your testimony on the importance of prayer. As we pray, our testimonies will be strengthened.

situations, scriptures, and songs

Repentance—Erin feels bad about lying to her mother about the stain on her Sunday dress. *GAK* no. 305, Enos 1:1–15.

Sing: "Help Me, Dear Father," *Children's Songbook,* 99

Family trials—Michael is worried about his older sister; she is skipping her church meetings and staying out late at night. *GAK* no. 321, Mosiah 27:8–23.

Sing: "Home," *Children's Songbook,* 192

Thanksgiving—Andrew has had a good day with his babysitter. It's time for bed, and she is not a member of the church. He feels awkward praying in front of her and doesn't think he has anything important to say tonight anyway. *GAK* no. 117, Daniel 6:10.

Sing: "Thanks to Our Father," *Children's Songbook,* 20

Knowledge—Sandy heard the prophet say that girls shouldn't have more than one set of earrings in their ears. She's been saving her money to get her ears pierced a second time for months. *GAK* no. 403, James 1:5–6, JS—H 1:14–20.

Sing: "The Sacred Grove," *Children's Songbook,* 87

Comfort—Molly's grandmother just died, and Molly doesn't understand why it had to happen. Molly's grandmother was her best friend. *GAK* no. 227, Matthew 26:36–45.

Sing: "I Need My Heavenly Father," *Children's Songbook,* 18

Help—Josh had studied all week for a science test, but now that he is taking the test he can't seem to remember anything he studied. He's scared he will fail. *GAK* no. 318, Ether 3.

Sing: "I Am a Child of God," *Children's Songbook,* 2–3

Missionary experiences—Adam's older brother just went on a mission to South Africa. He is getting to do all kinds of neat things, and he is teaching the gospel every day. Adam wishes he could have gone with his brother on his mission. *GAK* no. 310, Alma 17:9.

Sing: "Called to Serve," *Children's Songbook,* 174–75

19. Remember the sabbath Day

Children's Songbook, 155

Opening Song: "I Feel My Savior's Love," *Children's Songbook,* 74
Closing Song: "Remember the Sabbath Day," *Children's Songbook,* 155

Lesson Purpose

"I will serve God by doing things on the Sabbath that will help me feel close to Heavenly Father and Jesus" (*2008 Outline for Sharing Time and the Children's Sacrament Meeting Presentation,* 9).

Materials needed

- The Book of Mormon
- Church bulletin
- Display table and 2 large cloth coverings
- Family history sheet
- Flower
- Hammer
- Hymnal
- Journal
- Paint brush
- Pass-along Card
- Picture of a family
- Picture of a temple
- Small pillow
- Spinner from a family game, with numbers 1–4

Preparation

- Drape one cloth over the table so that it touches the floor in front and covers as much of the two sides as possible.
- Place the materials on the display table.
- The other cloth will be used to cover the items from the children's view.

Teaching suggestions

Introduce the words to this brief song, and have the children repeat them several times. Take time to discuss its important message with the children and help them understand why the Sabbath is kept holy. Let the children practice singing the song several times. When they are comfortable with it, divide the children into two groups, and help them try singing in a round. It helps to have a second person lead the children at first. The second group of children will begin to sing after the word "holy."

After they have practiced several times, show the children your display table. Tell them that the items on the table represent some of the things they can do on Sunday that will keep the Sabbath day holy and help them feel closer to Heavenly Father.

Show the children the items on your table, and talk about the way each item relates to an appropriate Sunday activity. Allow the children to share their own thoughts about how they could carry out this activity in their own lives.

After all of the items have been discussed, cover the display table, and let the children see how many of the items they can name from memory. Tell the children that they will play a memory game as they continue to practice the song they have learned. Show the spinner to the children, and explain the rules to the game. If the spinner shows a one or a two, the corresponding number of items will be secretly removed from the table and the children must guess which items are missing. If the spinner shows a three, the song "Remember the Sabbath Day" will be sung normally. If the spinner shows a four, the song will be sung in the form of a round.

Cover the table with your drape before removing the objects, and hide the objects on the floor under your table drape so that the children can't see what has been removed. Show the table again, and ask the children what is missing. Help them identify each missing item, and remind the children of the activity it represented as it is replaced. Play with the remaining time.

Close with a brief reminder of your testimony and how happy you are to have the Sabbath as a time to rest and come closer to Heavenly Father. Challenge the children to use some of the ideas they have discussed today to "Remember the Sabbath" and find ways to keep it holy.

objects and corresponding Activity

Picture of a temple—Visit a nearby temple's grounds.

Journal—Evaluate our lives, and make goals.

Church bulletin—Go to church.

Hammer—Give service (emphasize that this sometimes can mean physical work or it can be as simple as visiting someone sick or less active).

Family history sheet—Do genealogy.

Flower—Appreciate nature.

Picture of a family—Spend time with family.

Small pillow—Rest.

`al—Sing songs, and listen to music.

Book of Mormon—Read the scriptures.

Pass-along card—Share the gospel.

Paint brush—Explore talents.

20. "guess who" talks about service

Opening Song: " 'Give,' Said the Little Stream," *Children's Songbook, 236*
Closing Song: "Go the Second Mile," *Children's Songbook, 167*

Lesson purpose

"The prophets and apostles teach me how to serve" (*2008 Outline for Sharing Time and the Children's Sacrament Meeting Presentation, 9*).

Materials needed

- Individual pictures of Gordon B. Hinckley, Thomas S. Monson, James E. Faust, Russell M. Nelson, Jeffrey R. Holland, Henry B. Eyring, and David A. Bednar (available through Church Distribution)
- Chalkboard or other display area
- Tape or other fastener

Preparation

- Post the pictures of the Prophet and Apostles on the chalkboard.

Teaching suggestions

Ask the children if they know who the men are on the board. Allow them to identify anyone they know. Next, go through and identify each individual by name, let the children repeat them back to you.

Help the children understand that these men are prophets and apostles of the Lord, they lead and guide Heavenly Father's church today. Ask the children to share some of the things they think these men might tell them about following Jesus Christ and living the gospel. Allow them to share their answers.

Let the children know that they will be learning more about what these special men have said about service. You will give them hints about which man you will be talking about and they will try to guess which one he is. For the younger children, give hints about what the person looks like, colors he is wearing, and letters in his name until the children are able to identify him. For the older children, allow them to reverently ask you "yes" and "no" questions about the same sorts of details until the person is identified.

Choose which person to talk about in a random order. After he has been identified, remind the children of his name and position as you point out his picture. Share that person's quote about service and help the children discuss what they can learn from it. After it has been discussed, sing the corresponding song and then move on to the next individual. After all of the men have been identified and discussed, review their names with the children once again.

Close with your testimony of the Prophet and Apostles as well as the blessings of service. Challenge the children to take one thing that they talked about today and try harder to be of service in that manner during the coming week.

Quotes and Songs

Gordon B. Hinckley—"You want to be happy? Forget yourself and get lost in this great cause, and bend your efforts to helping people" (Church News, 9 Sept. 1995, 4).

Sing: "When We're Helping," *Children's Songbook*, 198

Thomas S. Monson—"I have tried to pattern my life after the Master, . . . Whenever I have had a difficult decision to make, or perhaps have had to measure the request to give a blessing against the endless demands of some of my paperwork, I have always . . . asked myself, 'What would He do?' Then I try to do it. . . . I can assure you the choice has never been to stay and do paperwork!" (Jeffrey R. Holland, "President Thomas S. Monson: Finishing the Course, Keeping the Faith," *Ensign*, Sept. 1994, 12–13).

Sing: "I'm Trying to Be like Jesus," *Children's Songbook*, 78

James E. Faust—"Following the Savior means overcoming selfishness; it is a commitment to serve others" (James E. Faust, "What's in It for Me?," *Ensign*, Nov. 2002, 19).

Sing: "I'll Walk with You," *Children's Songbook*, 140

Russell M. Nelson—"I have a deep and abiding faith in God and in his Son, Jesus Christ. The work I'm now engaged in is the most important cause in the world. It's all-encompassing, it's fulfilling, and it's challenging. And I must do my best, because I have an accountability for this stewardship" (Marvin K. Gardner, "Elder Russell M. Nelson: Applying Divine Laws," *Ensign*, Jun. 1984, 9).

Sing: "I Will Be Valiant," *Children's Songbook*, 162

Jeffrey R. Holland—"Our words, like our deeds, should be filled with faith and hope and charity . . . With such words, spoken under the influence of the Spirit, tears can be dried, hearts can be healed, lives can be elevated, hope can return, confidence can prevail" (Jeffrey R. Holland, "The Tongue of Angels," *Ensign*, May 2007, 16–18).

Sing: DeFord, Sally. "If the Savior Stood Beside Me," *Friend*, Oct. 1993, 14

Henry B. Eyring—"You must ask in faith for revelation to know what you are to do" (Henry B. Eyring, "Rise to Your Call," *Ensign*, Nov. 2002, 76).

Sing: "Tell Me, Dear Lord," *Children's Songbook*, 176

David A. Bednar—"You can increase in your desire to serve God (see D&C 4:3), and you can begin to think as missionaries think, to read what missionaries read, to pray as missionaries pray, and to feel what missionaries feel. You can avoid the worldly influences that cause the Holy Ghost to withdraw, and you can grow in confidence in recognizing and responding to spiritual promptings. Line upon line and precept upon precept, here a little and there a little, you can gradually become the missionary you hope to be and the missionary the Savior expects" (David A. Bednar, "Becoming a Missionary," *Ensign*, Nov. 2005, 44).

21. children all over the world

Children's Songbook, 16–17

Opening Song: "Holding Hands Around the World," *Friend,* July 2002, 44–45
Closing Song: "Children All Over the World," *Children's Songbook,* 16–17

Lesson Purpose

"Heavenly Father loves all of His children" (*2008 Outline for Sharing Time and the Children's Sacrament Meeting Presentation,* 9).

materials needed

- Chalkboard and chalk
- Large map of the world
- Tape or other fastener
- Copies of the following *Friend* articles:
  "Making Friends: Pili and Loli Romero Carrascoso of Seville, Spain," *Friend,* Oct. 1992, 42–43
  "Making Friends: Feleti Vimahi of Pangai, Tonga," *Friend,* Apr. 2004, 16
  "Making Friends: Gunar Grossman of Dresden, Germany," *Friend,* Mar. 1997, 20
  "Friends in Denmark," *Friend,* Oct. 1975, 28
  "Making Friends: Claire and Laurence Küsseling of Gournay, France," *Friend,* Jan. 2000, 15
  "Making Friends: Miyako Tashiro of Osaka, Japan," *Friend,* Aug. 2000, 41

Preparation

- Be familiar with each featured child's story.
- Copy and cut out a picture of the child from each *Friend* article. If illustrated copies of the *Friend* stories are unavailable, prepare large stick pins with each child's name on small paper flags.
- Become familiar with the pronunciations provided in the *Children's Songbook* for "thank you" in various languages.

Teaching suggestions

Ask the children to tell you some things that they can pray about and allow them to share their answers. Help them understand that saying thank you for all our many blessings is an important part of prayer. Help them make a list of things to be thankful for. Write their list on the chalkboard.

Next, introduce the children to the first section of the song, stopping at the piano interlude. Say the words with the children several times, and let them hear the melody and try singing along. Practice this portion of the song with the children until they are comfortable with the words.

Now post the map on the chalkboard. Help the children understand that this map shows the entire world. Point out where your Primary children live on the map, and tell them that you will introduce them to some children from other places in the world.

Show the pictures of the children, one at a time, in the order that their language is presented in the song. Share a few pieces of information about that child, the place where they live, and missionary efforts in their country.

Place the child's picture on the map at the country represented. Then teach the children how to say "thank you" in the language of that country. If stick pins are being used, gently poke it through the map, and simply let it dangle behind with just the flag and end showing from the front.

When all the pictures have been placed, review the order and pronunciation of each "thank you." Introduce the music, and sing the words to this portion of the song, ending with "we thank thee." Let the children practice this section, and add it to the first section that they learned. Add the last phrases of the song and practice the entire song several times.

Close by expressing Heavenly Father's love for all His children, and challenge your Primary children to look for opportunities to get to know others that might be from different places or cultures.

22. my body is a temple

Opening Song: "Hinges," *Children's Songbook,* 277
Closing Song: "The Lord Gave Me a Temple," *Children's Songbook,* 153

Lesson Purpose

"I am thankful for my body. I know my body is a temple" (*2008 Outline for Sharing Time and the Children's Sacrament Meeting Presentation,* 9).

materials needed

- Copies, on cardstock, of illustrations and song choices from this lesson
- *GAK* no. 403 or large picture of the First Vision
- The Holy Bible
- Container to hold song choices
- Empty trash can
- Large hand mirror
- Large sheet of butcher paper
- Tape or other fastener

Preparation

- Have a small child lay down on the butcher paper, trace his outline, and decorate it to look like a child.
- Cut the resulting picture into eleven pieces.
- Cut out and laminate the illustrations.
- Place the illustrations inside the container.

Teaching suggestions

Show the children the mirror you brought. Take the mirror around the room, giving the children a chance to look at their reflection. Ask several children to name something that they liked about what they saw. Provide some other ideas to reinforce theirs.

Remind the children that our bodies—and our lives—are gifts from Heavenly Father. We are His children, and we were created in His image. Show the children the picture of the First Vision to reinforce that Heavenly Father has a body just like theirs.

Read 1 Corinthians 3:16 with the children. Ask them what this verse says we are (temples). Heavenly Father expects us to treat our bodies with respect and to take care of them. Ask the children to share some ideas on how they can take care of and respect the bodies Heavenly Father gave them.

Show the children the container of choices and songs. Tell them that they are going to help you build a body that is healthy, clean, and pure by helping make choices that we make every day. These choices affect our bodies and spirits. There will also be songs to sing in the container that talk about our bodies or good choices that you can make for your body. A song or a good choice will be traded for a piece of the body puzzle; a bad choice will be thrown into the trash can you provide.

Close with your testimony that each of the children is a special child of God, and encourage them to treat their bodies with respect so that they can always remember how special they are to Heavenly Father.

Candy
Bar

"The Lord Gave
Me a Temple"
Page 153

"Head, Shoulders,
Knees and Toes"
Page 275

"The Word of
Wisdom"
Page 154

"I Am a
Child of God"
Page 2

"Do as I'm
Doing"
Page 158

"Hinges"
Page 277

"Healthy, Wealthy,
and Wise"
Page 280

23. Samuel Tells of the Baby Jesus

Opening Song: "Book of Mormon Stories," *Children's Songbook,* 118
Closing Song: "Samuel Tells of the Baby Jesus," *Children's Songbook,* 36

Lesson Purpose

"The prophecies were fulfilled. Jesus Christ was born and the righteous rejoiced" (*2008 Outline for Sharing Time and the Children's Sacrament Meeting Presentation,* 10).

Materials Needed

- Copies, front and back, of the word strips from this lesson (Make two copies of the word strips for the chorus.)
- *GAK* no. 314
- The scriptures
- Chalk and chalkboard

Preparation

- Write the words to the song on the board, leaving space for the word strips to be placed where the highlighted words are.
- Place the appropriate word strip with the scripture reference showing in each blank.
- For junior Primary, provide a list of the needed words at the bottom of the board to choose from.
- Review the story of Samuel's prophecy found in Helaman 13 and 14, and 3 Nephi 1:9–15.

Teaching Suggestions

Tell the children that the words on the board represent a very important prophecy that is found in the scriptures. When we read the scriptures we learn about things that have happened, and things that will still happen. We learn the messages that all the past prophets have prepared for us to hear.

Show the children the picture of Samuel. Ask them if they remember which prophet is being portrayed and what he might have said that they will be learning about today.

The children will help you fill in the blanks in this new song's lyrics and identify what important event is being talked about by reading their scriptures. Everywhere a scripture is posted in the song, a word is missing. If they will read the scripture, the children can figure out what word is missing.

Have the children begin with the first line and work through to the end of the song. Stop after every couple of phrases are completed. Repeat the words with the children. Introduce the melody, and allow the children to sing what they have learned to that point. When the entire song has been sung, go back and share the entire story of Samuel's prophecy with the children.

Close with your testimony of the importance of listening to the prophets' council. Testify that Heavenly Father will always keep His promises, and express your thankfulness for the birth of the Savior.

Lyrics and scripture References

"Said Samuel, 'Within **five** (Helaman 14:2) years A **night** (Helaman 14:3) will be as **day**' (Helaman 14:3)."

"And Baby **Jesus** (Matthew 1:21) will be born In a land far, far away."

"**Hosanna!** (Matthew 21:9) **Hosanna!** (Matthew 21:9) Oh, let us gladly **sing** (Psalm 96:1) How blessed that our Lord was born; Let earth receive her **King!** (Zechariah 14:9)."

"Across the sea, in **Bethlehem**, (Matthew 2:1) Lord **Jesus** (Matthew 1:21) came to earth As Samuel had prophesied, And **angels** (Luke 2:13) sang His birth."

"**Hosanna!** (Matthew 21:9) **Hosanna!** (Matthew 21:9) Oh, let us gladly **sing** (Psalm 96:1) How blessed that our Lord was born; Let earth receive her **King!** (Zechariah 14:9)."

Helaman 14:2

Helaman 14:3

Helaman 14:3

Matthew 1:21

Matthew 21:9

Matthew 21:9

Psalm 96:1

Zechariah 14:9

live

night

day

Jesus

Hosanna

Hosanna

sing

King

Matthew 2:1

Matthew 1:21

Luke 2:13

Bethlehem

Jesus

angels

24. Be a christmas Star

Opening Song: "Stars Were Gleaming," *Children's Songbook,* 37
Closing Song: "I Am like a Star," *Children's Songbook,* 163

Lesson Purpose

"Because I know that I am a child of God and that Jesus Christ is my Savior, I will . . ." (*2008 Outline for Sharing Time and the Children's Sacrament Meeting Presentation,* 10).

materials needed

- Copies, on cardstock, of the star illustrations (Make two copies for the lesson and enough for one star per child.)
- *GAK* no. 203
- 10 sandwich bags
- 10 small gift tags
- Chalkboard and chalk
- Clear packing tape
- Crayons or colored pencils
- Extension cord
- Glitter glue
- Glue
- Hole puncher
- Plastic storage bag
- Scissors
- Short Christmas tree
- Strand of large, outdoor Christmas lights (Be sure that each bulb will light independently of the others.)
- Strand of mini Christmas lights (Be sure that each bulb will light independently of the others.)
- Unsharpened pencil or wooden dowel
- Yarn or ribbon

Preparation

- Request permission to display the Christmas tree in your Primary room for the duration of the season.
- Before December arrives, compose a letter to the parents of the Primary children explaining the Light Challenge (see the example included at the end of this lesson), and distribute it to all the parents.
- Cut out four stars.
- Trace around the side and top edges of the blank side of one star with glue. Leave the bottom portion unglued. Place another star, message side up, on top of the star with the glue and let it dry. This will be used as your tree topper.
- Trace around all edges of the blank side of another star with the glue, and lay a strip of glue in the center of the star. Place one end of the pencil in the center of the star. Place another star, message side up, on top of the star with the glue and let it dry. This will be used as a conductor's baton.

- Decorate both glued star props with glitter as desired.
- Set up the Christmas tree in the front of the Primary room where it can be easily seen, but where the light cords will not interfere with movement in the room.
- Remove the bulbs from both strings of lights.
- Wrap the empty strand of small lights on the Christmas tree.
- Place the small lights in a plastic bag for storage.
- Place your star on the top of the tree.
- Write a song title and page number (from this lesson) on each gift tag.
- Place a song gift tag and a large bulb in each sandwich bag. Tape the bags under random children's chairs.
- Tape the outdoor light string across the top of the chalkboard. Use the extension cord to plug in these lights (make sure the cord is out of the way).
- After the Primary presentation, the extension cord will be used to light the tree during upcoming Primary meetings.

Teaching Suggestions

Share the picture of the Wise Men and discuss what they were following. What was the role of the star? It was to light the way and show the direction that the Wise Men needed to follow to find Jesus.

Help the children understand that they can be Christmas stars as well. When we give service to others, share our testimonies, or make righteous choices, we shine. Because the children know that they are children of God and that Jesus Christ is their Savior, they have a special light to share. Their light can help lead others to the gospel; it can help them remember to be like Jesus Christ.

Ask the children to help you find the bulbs for the string of lights you have on the chalkboard. The lights are hidden under some of the children's chairs. Each light also has a song for the children to sing. After all the bulbs have been found, select one child to come up and share his bulb and song with everyone. After the song is identified, ask the child who found it to choose a reverent friend (who didn't find a bulb) to help you direct the music using the star wand.

After the song is sung, help the children discuss what ideas it gave them for ways that they can shine. Write their thoughts on the chalkboard, and place the light on the string before moving to the next child and song.

Encourage the children to find opportunities to shine during the Christmas season. Help them understand that you will add a light to the Primary Christmas tree for every good deed the children perform.

Invite the children to cut out their own Christmas Star and write a goal for themselves on the back. Punch a hole in the top point, and help them string the star with ribbon to take home for their own Christmas tree.

Make sure every parent has access to the project letter!

suggested songs

"The Things I Do," *Children's Songbook,* 170

"I'll Walk With You," *Children's Songbook,* 140

" 'Give,' Said the Little Stream," *Children's Songbook,* 236

"I'm Trying to Be like Jesus," *Children's Songbook,* 78

"Smiles," *Children's Songbook,* 267

"When We're Helping," *Children's Songbook,* 198

"Family Prayer," *Children's Songbook,* 189

"Go the Second Mile," *Children's Songbook,* 167

"Our Primary Colors," *Children's Songbook,* 258

"Have a Very Merry Christmas!" *Children's Songbook,* 51

I can Be a christmas star!

Dear Parents,

This Christmas season we would like to encourage our Primary children to shine with the light of Christ by finding ways to give service and show love for others around them. They have been challenged to become "Christmas Stars." Their efforts will be acknowledged in Primary. Each week we will share the names and tasks performed by the children and add a light to our Christmas tree for each act of kindness.

Please watch for and provide opportunities for your children to shine in their own special ways over the coming weeks. When a good deed is noticed, please call, or e-mail a member of the Primary presidency or send a note with your child on Sunday. We will share their accomplishments and add lights to our tree during our opening exercises each week in December.

May your family have a joyful Christmas season!

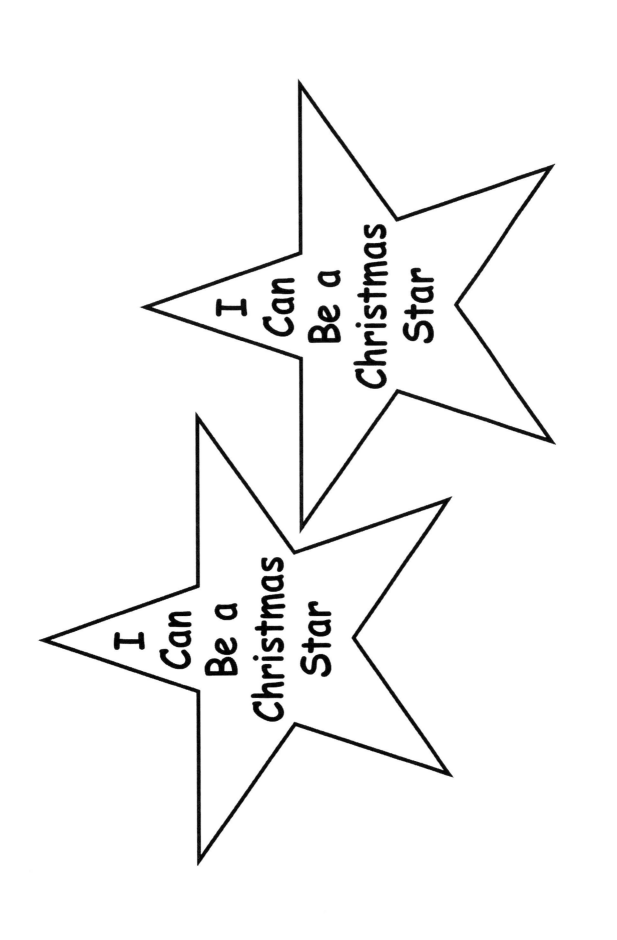

I Can Be a Christmas Star

I Can Be a Christmas Star

About the Author

ALISON PALMER is a lifelong member of the Church. Born in Mesa, Arizona, she grew up in West Virginia and graduated from Marshall University with a bachelor's degree in nursing.

Alison has held many callings in the Church, including several that have helped develop her great love for the Primary children. She has served as nursery leader, pianist, chorister, teacher, den leader, and Primary president. She has also taught Sunday School and served as a teacher and leader in Relief Society and Young Women organizations.

Writing is Alison's favorite pastime, but you can frequently find her reading, playing piano, cooking, attending the temple, taking long walks, sewing, or playing with her family.

Alison is the author of *Sharing through Primary Songs, Volumes One, Two, and Three*; *Special Occasion: Sharing Through Primary Song*; *Planting Seeds of Faith: Fun Character-building Activities for LDS Children*; and *Walking the Path of Faith: More Fun Character-building Activities for LDS Children*.

You can learn more about Alison at
WWW.AMPALMER.COM